University of Love
part 1

Tom Fry

Pi Brand Books
London, UK

First published 2018
Amazon Books
This edition 2021

Copyright © Tom Fry, 2018

For a bird
untrapped

Contents

Prologue: Home is Where the Heart isn't

part 1
    Converging on Anger

1: Further Education
2: Music College
3: Xenophobe
4: The Scottish Problem
5: Splurge
6: Buddha and the Tortoise
7: Help Desk
8: Floristry
9: Defloristation

part 1a
    Summary of Solipsism

10: Gracelessland
11: Heartbreak Hole
12: Working it out
13: Brewer's Droop

Prologue: Home is Where the Heart isn't

My girlfriend had turned eighteen a couple of days before me, I'd gone over the top on gifts; painting a violin in the union flag, spending all my money on a bunch of crap she really didn't want, boxes within boxes within boxes, lots of crêpe paper. Expensive chocolates for her folks, wrapped by the shop with fancy ribbons of purple and orange. When challenged by her father for being overtly political, I gawped in dumbfounded amazement.

On the eve of *my* eighteenth birthday, I captained a team to world championship glory in a local Sussex game: Toads. At the stroke of midnight, the landlord, on our team, invited me to leap across the bar to pull my first legal pint, the tenth of the evening.

The next day, with my first legal hangover, I voted against the Tories in *the* landslide election of a generation. You're welcome.

That same week, girlfriend and girlfriend's friends organised a combined party between a bunch of us, camping in a country garden field with a swimming pool. I thought we might have sex, but no. A surprise cake, made into the shape of a pair of shorts remains the highlight. Sadly, I'd not been able to enjoy any of it through an alcohol-fueled flush of fuck-it.

Saddened and maddened by every single little bloody thing, *including* friends, for sanity's sake, false jollity consumed me. False *fricking* jollity; forced fun, nauseating plastic insincerity with jazz hands, woohoo, six hour's tricky conversation ignored, lost in hurt, faking it to breaking point, hiding floods of tears, laughing fart oo loudly hah as memory skewers stab the ears, grimacing under thunder, corrupt connection, set to broadcast old comedy repeats, befuddling firmly to refuse unwanted care, lacking the skill to course-correct conversation's inexorable pull toward the black hole of an unspoken lie.

Are you alright? *Uh?* Are you alright? *What?* You just phased out there. *Oh,* I'm fine thanks. Are you sure? Ahahahahaha, yeah I'm good, cheers, ahahahahahem. Really? Haha, yep, absolutely fine, thank you, ahahahahem. Is something wrong? Hahahaha, no, ahahaha. Okay, well, if you're sure. Haha, certain, thanks, hehehe, isn't weather great? Well, yeah, quite, in fact, I *just* asked why you won't take your tee-shirt off, it's so hot and everyone else is naked, and *you* jumped in with all your clothes on, so, hello, *hellowo*, you there? *Uh?* Are you alright? *What?* You just phased out, oh, you're a dick. Ahahahahahaha? No, you're a dick.

A youth orchestra tour next up, boys and girls to play away. First day abroad, wallet lost. Slit emotionally; throat to anus, turned inside out doing nasty things for bet money, or beer. Thirsty days, long warm evenings, scrounging any dreg. On the last night, overwrought, 'alcohol poisoning' ensued, having a fit in a foreign ambulance, electrical sensors over my bare torso.

Home. Driving test passed, *soberly* did I ferry myself to and fro, for a fab fortnight, finding far-flung friends in the family Fiat. Parents away, one bad choice; to drive drunk, or to sleep outside. I crashed, badly. Goodbye Fiat, farewell newfound freedoms. Hello remorse, guilt, penitence, and apology. And punishment. Grounded: no booze, no fun, oh, and also, no girls. I didn't mind *that* much, what ground away most of all was being allowed out.

So, I saw cuntychops again, working for *him* at *his* jazz club; he'd phoned on the landline as parents hovered, offering a place in the house band for some guest boogie-woogie piano-shakers on half-a-dozen late-night high-energy shows over the summer; too numb to react, too stupefied to shout, taciturn, I agreed. Within the terrible shadow world of silence, I felt he owed me a courtesy or two and gigs *were* my favoured currency. Absurd as it may seem, I was *grateful* to him for the opportunity. Moderately grateful. I wasn't happy though, oh no, feverishly fucking furious was I, incandescent with eye-popping lividity.

Distrustful of drinks, watching every drop of liquid from tap to lip, I'd ask for a different glass, no, not that one, *that* one, down the freshly poured pints, and then play until my fingers were in tatters, not wanting to unclench the face or delay playing for a single moment, in case I'd inadvertently catch his eye.

The familiar smoky room, long and thin, tucked in, double-bass behind the grand-piano, in front of the drum-kit. So many bad memories, and yet, not quite enough to have me running out screaming, as I was ready to do. I'd planned my escape, where to put my instrument, off stage, how I'd hit him with an uppercut and then wrestle him to the ground and smash his fucking face in until I could smash no more, then run, fly down the stairwell feet first at any who got in my way, out that door, that *damned* door.

Will you be staying for a lock in? No bloody way am I staying for a lock in thank you very much, there's no way I'm having that door locked with me this side of it, *ever* again. Sorry, what? *Uh?*

Music passed in a physical assault on the senses, all new, mostly simple, nothing too hard. Blues in C, and-a-one two three. Brain pain allaying much actual pain, by gig's end, on the right hand, blood-blisters would distend the index and middle fingers from the tips behind the nails, down all three segments of flesh, puffing up across the knuckles, over the metacarpophalangeal join onto the top of the palm, the inside of the thumb, and ring-finger tip too. Bad news when blisters burst mid-gig. Very bad. Messy. Pussy. Bloody. Slippery. Soft layers removed, scooped out, never to be seen again. Kept playing though, that's the job.

The left had cramping and contact issues of its own, index, middle and pinky, bruised and bent, rheumatoid arthritis pending. In hindsight, for a troubled mind under duress, beating and clamping swollen knuckles repeatedly against solid ebony, grating exposed fingertip nerve endings across high-tension wire at 190bpm, was blessed distraction from an inability to breathe with the concentrated hatred bubbling away in the lungs.

The last such hateful boogie-woogie gig was for some musical MPs after conference. Television Whoever, came with cameras. The following day, footage appeared on the local news for a few seconds or more, my poor hardworking fingers mostly obscured by subtitle headline text, but there it stood, undeniably, success, the well-honed image of my younger self, wearing shades and funking out in a jazz club, transmitted forever across the galaxy. Cool. I'm cool. The furthest horizon reached, the last tick box ticked, as a teen. Hurrah! Proof captured, stored for evermore on a lost VHS tape.

Being on TV was a big thing back then, much as it is now, perhaps even more so, exactly the kind of thing a lad with my aspiration should have wanted; *had* wanted. Inside, nothing, breathless, a small wholly hollow triumph. Familial elations witnessed with no satisfaction. Overly-affectionate squeals from watching the boy-man-pet doing energetic things with a double-bass, once my very reason to show off and needle for their attention, sat as a blank dullness in a clay mind. Their open pride and joy, which should've prompted grinning, brought interminable glumness and, ultimately, at least on the face of it, a selfish grumpy teenage arsehole. Where love should've been lay a surly sullen sunken void, no pretence to be grateful, wallowing happily, unhappy in the sharp biting wash of self-pity.

The family remained unaware of the manager's transgression. One day, maybe, but not yet, we had religious truth's truth to tackle first. Between us, many words were already insults, many *many* words, so *very* many words that it was slow work to get conversation to where we were able to say anything much at all. Interference sat on the line such that communications had been severed, mere static noise with the volume up. Taking their hardcore material sacrifices for granted, I couldn't help but be deeply upset that they wouldn't stop praying for me, certain proof of prayer's futility kept *fairly* well hidden from them. Ahahaha.

UNIVERSITY OF LOVE

UNIVERSITY OF LOVE

part 1

Converging on Anger

UNIVERSITY OF LOVE

1: Further Education

When it was time to leave Sussex, I was very happy to go, monocultural boy hits multicultural fan, splat; with childhood's restraints unlocked, stony reality of self-determination dawning, I grew up blinkingly fast with a lot to think about. Don't we all?

A vibey Yorkshire music college had accepted me, and *I, them*, sure, I'd 'classical' offers from 'good' London colleges, (double-bass, easy,) but, they'd just not seemed quite far enough away. Life itself would only last a year, or less, definitely, definitely definitely; I just knew. No imagined future, no career planned, no aspiration for a proper qualification, so I chose to 'study' jazz.

Enthusiastic, but no prodigy, as a classically trained double-bassist, jazz excited me. Unknown order within chaos, and vice versa. Joining now with now, bass thumping time, all the time.

I *loved* jazz. Jazz meant playing. I *loved* playing. Playing turned off the world. Click. Swim. Click. Laughter and applause.

Classical music, however, for a bull-fiddler, passes slowly contemplating the navel, counting multi-rests waiting to play, two, three, four, forty-one, two, three, four. In stuffy rooms, earnest conductors working on difficult sections with the violins, brass and woodwind, and percussion, on tacet bass sections, filled the long hot summer afternoons of youth with a deep and profound resentment. In my idyllic abyss, visions of life passing without action and distraction were simply insufferable, so, self-indulgently and for lack of better options: jazz. Far away jazz.

Academically, despite best efforts to sabotage exams with alcoholism, required grades had been scraped to the letter, so I qualified, just, by age and poor results, for the last year of state-subsidised degree-level tutelage in England, in Yorkshire, in *jazz*. Hah! Fools. Destiny was on my side. Death would be joyous.

The parents had kindly agreed to stump up for rent until schooling finished, so, for lodgings I moved directly into a house; a large rotten ramshackle terraced house of six people, three boys, three girls. I was going to die in this house, it was decided.

My ground-floor bedroom sash window, with rusty iron bars on the outside, had been painted shut, with two panes broken when I'd arrived. Some helpful person had inexpertly taped cardboard over it, blocking out much of the natural light, yet still letting in much of the cold. With no practical ventilation, except the door into the hallway to the kitchen, the smell of rot was only overpowered by burnt toast, ashtrays and unshowered teenager. It mattered not, I didn't care, no one I loved would ever see it.

One of the new housemates was a music friend from Sussex who'd been in the family Fiat when I'd crashed it, drunk, through fifteen metres of chain-link fencing, and a telegraph pole, in a naïvely careless risk to our mortality. He never let me forget, just him and his face. Indignity stunned me speechless. He knew stuff, I knew that he knew stuff, he knew that I knew he knew stuff, and we both knew that I didn't want everyone finding out. We had an unspoken bond that sat behind serious eyebrows when things got a little bit tetchy.

He did everything in his power to inspire and cheer me, chivvying and cajoling at every opportunity. He introduced me to the main university campus, where people were, all the action occurred, and subsidised beer poured freely. A reliable wingman for a convivial drinking pilot, it seemed a reasonable exchange of favours. Happy not to think, and extremely glad of a friend who knew his way about, I followed him blindly to weekly events, wormed my way into the union bar and leeched his social life until I found friends of my own. Officially, music college boys, such as I, weren't really allowed access to university goings-on, but, as wingman, doors opened wide. In return, I'd distract the ugly ones, that was the deal.

Rag week was a disco of opportunity. Everywhere one turned was another eager segment of society colourfully and noisily exercising their right to be recognised. Enthusiasts fought for the best tree-branches and wall-spots to spout their hearty truths. Photocopied posters covered every wall-space, banners blazed, ballasted balloons blew, stickers stuck, tins and sabres rattled.

Student life opened wide myopic curious eyes to realms of unalike thinking, no subject or opinion seemed too outrageous to be beyond the pooling of perspective, principles proliferated in teeny-weeny minds. Mine was full and clogged instantly. Looped mindknots of previously unthought thoughts clotted the neural processors, inhibiting the carefree fun expected.

It was widely known, at least to me, that, in public, no one ought talk about; sex, religion or politics. Them's the rules. Well, no such luck. With so many new people to accidentally insult all round and about, it was impossible to know who'd defend any particular stance, or the degree to which they'd stand up and fight their corner. Sentences became minefields while pandering to the shifting linguistic bounds of societal obligation. So, I opened my heart up to social justice, taking great cares to refine my language to stop arbitrarily offending others. Exorcising my right to be recognised as a pig-ignorant yokel, with constant reference and deference to peculiar keyhole visions of acceptability, it seemed best, ordinarily, just to say nothing, never make jokes at anyone's expense, ever, and refrain from affecting funny foreign inflection for fear of offending frail Frenchmen. I, for one, boggled at how a single brain could process all the conflicting data in one lifetime. Alongside my death wish, there didn't seem much point trying to get a grip on what *other* people thought, *their* problems *their* own, but, life persists, so, efforts were made to absorb the etymology of the long list of truly offensive words that the rag-week hand-book said not to use, ever, many of which were entirely new to me.

On campus grounds, gay rights, in particular, were being shouted about loudly. Under such a potent onslaught of bright confident happy people, my own chaste misgivings towards sex-out-of-wedlock crumbled like wet biscuit. Empathy: Lesson one. Other people are people too, *all* other people. Om.

I coveted the free and easy way in which they stuck two fingers up at the scriptures, with such a lack of fear of retribution from petty Gods. Lucky buggerers. My God still had me trapped, in fear of breaking a moral code that He still refused to describe in any great detail. Like them, I wanted to tell the world how much I particularly wanted to express myself through sex, only, there was no 'coming out' as straight, no soapbox from which to shout, no flag or gazebo to stand under, no tee-shirt to promote straightness without a misconstrued homophobic undercurrent. No one would ever propose a straight pride festival; given all of history, and that, it seemed a rather trifling quibble.

Welcome strangers, passing by with glossy leaflets, brought awareness to the brutal suppression and vile treatment of women, homosexuals, the religious, and various down-trodden peoples of the world. Important stuff. Terrible stuff.

As an especially fresh freshman, to witness such passion on tricky subjects was invaluable for the inner schoolboy to learn and grow, emulating earnest language, copying willful behaviour, noticing courage of conviction and vital vehemence of spirit. although I struggled blinkeredly to understand what a double-bass playing student living on debt could do about any of it.

It felt vaguely disingenuous wandering from group to group agreeing with everyone about everything, but, in an equal world, if another person felt strongly enough about something to shout about it, then, who was I to deny them their position? I wanted to enjoy all the people I met and take in my surroundings gladly, in case of sudden death, which is what I was half-expecting to happen, any, moment, now.   Now.   Now...

Inner peace. Plenty to ponder. Solace could be found in the somewhat Buddhist mantra that; *most* people are *mostly* correct in the thrust of *most* of what they say, *most* of the time, even hippies. So, while the mind whirred endlessly, not quite able to answer cleverly or run away, I nodded through much testament there could be no possibility of my having a valid opinion upon and signed lots of heartfelt petitions I'm not sure that I really agreed with, some of which *clearly* didn't agree with each other. Empathy: Lesson two. People are complex. Om.

Drifting about, private worries and needs were drowned out, lost in a sea of martyrs clinging to some crusade or another. Somehow, in my humourless distrustful state, it felt like these various activists and compassionate bullies demanded of myself, and everyone, that we should stop treating them equally and, instead, raise up their singular troubles in stature above our own so that they may be heard the loudest, much like guitarists.

Before long, bored with fraudulent *bonhomie* beneath brash bombardment, brazen bouts of belligerence began to manifest. No room left in my bristling brain for any more of life's victims; one was quite enough. If the sole purpose of a new interaction was to be a spreading and storing of another's pain and distress as a personal memory, I really really *really* didn't want to know, thanks for the kindly offer though.

Unwelcome strangers passing with leaflets brought brutal self-awareness to how very little I cared. I'll take your flyer, and your pamphlet, and yours, sure, I'll take yours too, and yours, but, actually, why don't you save us all a lot of time and effort, the litter bin is over there.

It was all too easy to feel 'got at' in my municipal of mind. Violations? Colonialism? Colon violation? Why don't you talk to the gays about that? I'd mutter angrily, as I mooched through the banner-strewn university campus, chafing under a double entendre, furrowing a deepening groove to the music college.

UNIVERSITY OF LOVE

2: Music College

Famed for vibey jam-sessions with brilliant northern jazzers in its popular bustling late-night bar, the music college, due to some finance issue, and modern hygiene standards, had newly moved, inconveniently, away from all the decent student action to the other side of town, into an obnoxious newbuild brickbox that reeked sickeningly of chemical fumes and unwashed youth.

Some distracted architect must've held a grudge against those who'd be using this building, it had clearly been designed by an idiot, or, more probably, a community of idiots. The practice-rooms, for instance, 'specially designed' by an 'acoustic-engineer' had no sound insulation, yet the walls had been angled so that even soft sounds would cut the ears in peaky throbbing slaps of phasing interference. Drums were very painful, cymbals caused lasting injury. To top that: all windows, in all rooms, in all weathers, had to remain firmly shut, not even a crack, due to noise pollution and being located next to a busy working theatre. One could open the windows, but only when *not* playing music, *in a music college.* The heady bouquet of damp clammy mammals choked the sinuses once while the bleachy vomity paint smells had stopped stinging the eyes and throat. Smoking outside.

The unsubsidised mezzanine café-bar, which also served as the main meeting area for everyone, didn't allow live music in it, *in a music college.* We couldn't believe it. Instead, the sterile, drafty, and often *wet* space, in which they served alcohol, mainly to teenagers, had steep stairs in the centre that fell away sharply. Taking half-pint bets on bruise, blood or bone casualties made for macabre entertainment on rainy days. Uncomfortable low-slung seating had pensive students hunched over expensive drinks in chilly contemplation of career-ending injury.

Music lessons supplied much needed distraction from the off-putting environment. We had some great teachers, the very best imparters of knowledge and enthusiasm for harmonic growth that the 'world' had to offer, but the few short hours of classes each week were much earlier and less helpful than expected.

Advanced Theory, Harmony, and Composition lessons were, at least at first, remedial, which was a shame. Some of us were already able to read music, some of us weren't; some of us could play our instruments, some of us couldn't; some knew what the teacher was on about, some didn't; some could decipher chord symbols and charts, knew lots of jazz standards, had a history of group performance and were willing to play at any time with anyone, anywhere, for any reason, and some of us weren't.

All the students were at different stages along the musical path, obviously, many much further along it than myself, some had never stepped foot upon it, so, to make sure everyone could keep up, we began from square one. That's fairness, that is, in a *required-attendance,* trudging through town in biting drizzle before dawn to be told what a 'crotchet' is, kind of a way. An exactly equal education. The tutors had good stuff in their brains, useful stuff, chromatic revelations, but they weren't forthcoming, and so started a bitterly slow year for our group to learn that a twelve-bar blues has twelve bars in it, still, I'd made no other life plans.

To my horror, we were expected to write essays *about* jazz. Writing? Seriously? With these blisters? Life skills? No, thanks. Interest in lessons waned, history didn't matter, that'll come, or not, I simply wanted to play, presently. Playing music brought light, no time to wallow in darkness, reactive only to notes and banter thrown about. Eyes tightly shut, hidden behind a double life, lost in colourful swirls that smeared irrelevant thoughts away. Hours, days and weeks would pass in blissful candy-pop dreams, until instantly the biting chill of stark stinking reality would snap back in. Keep the groove, keep the groove, keep the oh.

Hanging out in the vibeless bar with half a pint and a double-bass, plenty of positive people popped up, prepared to prattle on about specific particulars of jazz harmony, solo flow, instrument technique, choice complex chord changes, scales, modes and favourite forms. Suddenly, reasons to stay alive flocked around. Jazz paradise. Nearly everyone needed a half-reasonable double-bass player. With little effort, I'd become a desirable commodity. It felt great, every twenty minutes filled with something new, responsive, and exciting to deal with. Without really thinking, I'd joined a bunch of bands and found myself merrily running about at the whim of a crazy rehearsal schedule for dynamic strangers. Empathy: Lesson three. Some people are brilliant. sOme.

Diary space suddenly at a premium, no time or *need* to think, just turn up and play, like children. Strange and glorious music filled the clammy practice rooms, bedrooms, lounges, hallways, *anywhere*, except my shit house. Wherever I lugged that double-bass, there would always be a musician or two, prepared to spend an hour or two going through favoured tunes, usually after a glass of water and, maybe, a cigarette outside, any excuse to get wet armpits into a breeze. Physically, fingertips were raw, hands bruised, wrists aching, forearms tender, shoulders sore, back niggled with exertion, belly constantly ravenous, fueled by potted pasta and cheap crisps, fatigue had set in deep, I stank like a baked-bean bolognaise, but this was living, really living.

However, no profound answers could be found when playing, nor smoking on doorsteps, nor ranting at baffled jazzers over cups of strong unsugared milkless tea, no amount of discussion of, say, diminished scales, or appropriate use of a flat-thirteenth, in over-priced cafés, would ever help answer the intense nagging questions and emotional predicaments that consumed the mind. Philosophically, no matter how many hours spent distracted by music making; no matter how many miles lumbering along grumbling self-righteously, I was getting nowhere fast.

UNIVERSITY OF LOVE

3: Xenophobe

Yorkshire was going to be a fantastic place to die. I bumbled about blithely, grinning manically in a cheery upbeat fashion, eyes on the next social event horizon, living for the moment, thrilled to be wedging distance between past and present, relishing the architecture, the crowds, the bars, sniffing flowers, enjoying insects, counting blessings, saying determinedly how good things were, how gladdening it felt to be here on this rock, in this place, at this time, how lucky we were. Come on world, let's have *fun*. Bootstraps grasped firmly, destination: altitude. Positive attitude. Goodly mood. Grinny grin. Groovy groove.

Bad move. For, for many loud social progressives, whose jet-set horizons commanded deference from us young impressionables, there existed a misplaced rage against contentment itself. Folks tolerating their fates were berated or faced weighty debates. Show up, get shown up, show down, get shot down. And repeat. Simply by assuming the accepting position, while attempting to spread sunniness and love to all, I'd unwittingly become the unthinking uncaring ambassador of the cultural oppressor. Who'd've known? Not *I*. Maybe I really was more abrasive than memory allows, maybe my version of jollity tinged with pathos and mild self-hatred fell outside the bounds of normal humour, whatever, it wasn't long before I'd learned the error of my ways; the spread of false jollity: follity, if you will, is pure folly.

Due to past and pending political problems, proud patriotism was perceived as a practice of the poor and stupid. But, but, but *I'm* poor and stupid. Passed about were allegations of willful ignorance being equivalent to wanton criminal negligence, being counterpart to conspiratorial warmongering, being murder.

It is amazing what caffeine can do to a sadist.

Whenever stuck in conversation with such a person, either: one soon loathed oneself for one's silent ignorant responsibility in a long history of warring families, one hated oneself for being powerless to stop the strong eating the weak, one hated oneself for naïvely bending the truth in an attempt to make things seem more agreeable, or one hated oneself for being in the presence of such a vile creature, who'd insist that one hated oneself, whatever one's ambitions were or one's previous actions proved. I'd never known such self-contempt before and didn't care for it much; I'd been trying to let go of self-contempt, if anything. Empathy: Lesson four. Some people aren't brilliant. sOmany.

As a sound-bite, 'intolerance of the intolerable', provided a communal, national and international gold-standard for every personal freedom. No one need listen to offensive strangers. That's part of the bargain in a free society, people can vote with their feet, as at jazz gigs. Off I'd wander under dark clouds, struggling with a heavy internal umbrella, entirely unable to do anything about anything, least of all these moaning minnies.

Oft I'd wonder that things were, things are, things change mainly for the better, whysoever complain? Infancy and idiocy, war and peace, bloodshed and remorse, cruelty and kindness, common sense and civil sense, common law and civil law, civilisation, refinement, revolution, evolution, progress, due process, capital punishment finally a bygone horror, and now, multiculturalism in action, our very freedoms to be guaranteed, not all of the world had come so very very far.

With a reasonable free education system, free health service, free internet on its way; freedom from guns, freedom from natural disasters, deadly diseases, predators and sudden death, (except; Adders, and several varieties of poisonous mushroom that might do the job,) equal liberties for all, to shout about themselves through whistling megaphones, coming along nicely, Yorkshire, specifically, was perfect, despite the incessant drizzle.

Northern folk generally made for a pleasant enough populace or so it seemed through soft southern eyes. There existed a national togetherness, or near enough, comedic banter thrown about instead of arrows and bayonets, making for a peaceable peacetime, hard won by a long shared interwoven history of absurd wars, despotic kings and mad governors. Truce, through democratic insistence that none should be forced to put up with barbaric nonsense, a general agreement of what constitutes such nonsense historically, and an acceptance to adhere to the expanding body of scientific data that will continue to search out, in ever finer detail, *that* which nonsense itself actually *is*, helped by universal schooling and forced liberalisation of the general populace, folks like me, at the rate that such an elaborate scheme allows for. Drip drip. Hooray.

Even if no student really knew the true letter of the law, with the infamous 'golden-rules' binding us together in common peaceful purpose, we could be proud of the ever-changing jigsaw of general sensibilities that loosely defined us culturally, and united and protected us constitutionally. In the name of art, especially, everyone was allowed to do anything they wanted to try to get away with, almost, short of actual criminal damage, realisation of one's imagination limited only by one's charm, the financial force one wielded, or the height of one's tree.

How very lucky we were. What a marvelous time to be alive, if that's your thing. Just look at all the lovely people doing anything they want, enjoying their freedom to the fullest. Bravo. Just look at the sophisticates complaining resentfully about the very state of grace in which they are allowed to complain. Boo. Some people can be most ungrateful. Not me. Not patriotic scum, like me. In some ways, 'xenophobe' being leveled as a hippy insult, as something to be ashamed of, made me feel as though I were the only person around with a brain in my head, and, in some other ways, like the only person without one.

Society looked healthy from where I stood, it just seemed a bit odd why some people, who reaped its every advantage, acted like they wanted to dismantle it all from the bottom up, at the very moment when the full benefit of prolonged learning from well-documented errors seemed to be finally taking effect.

Hippies complained a lot about the free press, they still do, there's a lot to complain about; evil has all too often been given a soapbox, and the merest whiff of atrocity can spin nations into a wild frenzy, it's fair enough to moan, a bit, but even so, the free presses stoke the fires of nonsense-spotting, bellowing the good, stamping out the bad, keeping public debate vigorous. To those bad at maths, and equally unused to newspaper tricks, when statistics transmuted into bold hyper-excitable headlines it might've seemed as if we lived in the worst place in the world, when, really, by allowing scandal to be brought to everyone's shocked attention, by displaying failures of thought for all to see, by forcing hot topics down throats until changes happened, free speaking societies weren't failing to deal with their thorny issues, quite the opposite. But it took time. Change always took time. More time than I had to give, now mere months and counting.

I'd never be the great man once dreamed into being, I'd never take on the rotten institutions, theocracies, corrupt office. *I* couldn't get it together enough to understand anything fully, because around every corner there'd always be a pedantic arsehole attempting to derail trains of thought by throwing chains of irrelevant meaning across the tracks of reasonable conversational scope. The bastards. Words of power and import would have to be left to the academics, politicians, journalists, authors, songwriters and poets, maybe poets, I'd nothing to add to the great lexicon. I'd found my level, distilling the overwhelming into handy manageable sound-bites of simple instruction. If it's good enough for the free press, desk-diaries, all Buddhist philosophy, and most other religious texts, then it's plenty good enough for me.

4: The Scottish Problem

My girlfriend had moved to Scotland to study. I still loved her *very* much, to the point of obsessive hysterical possession. She was all I had. All I wanted. All my heart desired. All I allowed myself to think or talk about. Critically, we were still waiting.

Majestic family futures we'd defined in detail at the start of our relationship left us with dozens of promises to keep or break. Keenly had I tied myself to the restrictions of our plans, but then those best-laid plans had been, quite literally, buggered.

I often phoned her student halls. Too often. Bills became a worry. Weekly budgets wasted waiting querulously, quietly, impatiently, for a randomised Scottish student to announce that she wasn't, in actual fact, around. No need to rub it in, I thought. I'd had invisible friends before, most unsatisfactory.

When she *did* answer, I found myself confounded, flustered and frustrated at her lack of enthusiasm. Admittedly, yearning to be in her thoughts as often as she filled mine was acutely slim hope indeed, but I craved equivalence. It hurt that she wasn't equally crippled by our distant love, so I'd fish for assurances, pushing her to be similarly neurotic. Go on, say it, *I'll* say it, I lo... Words didn't come easily. I rarely knew the real meaning of most sounds flying out of the mouth or into the ears. Half of all inference was feeling. More than half. Probably more than that. Raw uproar and passion, where faith, hope and love abide, and psychosis, also. Several times we ended our chats with: well, we'll just have to wait and see what happens then, won't we? Clkuuuuuuuuuuuuuuuuuuuuuuuuuuuuuuuulloveyouuuuuu. Sniff. Which, in some ways, is simply horrendous, in other ways, a test, a challenge to be noble, or, possibly, a free-ticket kindly given, certainly a most stultifying moral dilemma for a horny teenager.

Sadness filled the flesh; so much sadness I reveled in it and wrapped myself in its cold embrace, hoping it'd take me one step closer to the end. Nnnnngh, okay, fine, next time, when *next* on the phone, *then;* death by broken heart on the hallway stairs.

Being left to fend for oneself in a new town persists as a very romantic notion and all; start a new life, settle down, create a family, build a home, a shed, something for a determined youngster to get eager teeth into, however, while enduring an empty bed under the onslaught of five noisy nymphomaniacs and thin walls, whilst she remained so very very far distant, for *some* reason the promised thrill of adventure escaped me.

She'd no plans to visit for she was busy, and nor would her student halls allow for me to stay, and she'd said not to go, also, which smarted a bit. Forcing myself upon her after a spoken 'no' was not on. I knew that. I'd been told. But, in my head, looking back bleakly, or forward forlornly, darkness covered the skyline. I mused upon her, upon us, upon choices generally, our bonded psychic union as warm sunshine upon closed eyelids.

Starry-eyed isolation had the brain in overdrive, grandiose plans were crafted to turn up and propose with a platinum ring, roses, champagne, hotel-suite and romance. Say 'no' to *that*. Except I'd no ring or roses, no champagne, no way to transform plans into reality. Trains and hotels *way* too costly, no time to return in a day by bus, banned from driving, the long cold walk to Scotland the only option to allow the potential sowing of wild Oates. Sleeping rough on a Scottish street in winter appealed in *one* way, the unrequited romance of a sad, silent, frozen death.

Restless on grubby bed-sheets, failing to sleep, smoking cigarettes irritably, I'd cry a lot, like a man, a normal man, a teenage man, arguing all night with her, and God, in a pleading, huffy, puffy-headed whimper, snivelling into the pillow, grizzling until tupperware-skies meant leaving the house with weighty double face and fool's golden smile to continue the chirpy charade.

Still no ambition, no future plans as such, a jazzer meanwhile, as rubbish an example of humanity as existed anywhere, conviction grew that she needed her freedom from me, easily as much as I did. I still missed her, but now *required* reassurance, or closure. Wise girl housemates advised face-to-face only for closure. I agreed reticently, phone calls had become painful, my language skills insufficient for such a harrowing ordeal.

She decided to stay in Scotland for Christmas, so that answered that. Perceptions askew, options few, doubts nagged away, assurance wasn't forthcoming. Follity and love. Bumble along humming. There didn't seem much point to 'ought else; I'd definitely be dead by summer. Definitely definite.

Time drudged on, winter passed, cherry blossoms bloomed, hollow promises resonated. Head full of nonsense, ears full of noise, sap rising fast, the eyes opened wide to the abundance of girls, hundreds, thousands, but none special enough to replace *her* in my mind, after all, we were, at the end of the day, waiting, together, to be, potentially, married. It's a certain life-choice. Certain. If one stays pure of spirit, at least one will have always had that to be glad about. Thankfully, at some point soon, while still chaste, still eligible for heaven, the ribcage would explode and bloody innards burst asunder, poisoned by the venom of embittered loneliness, any, moment, now. Now.   Now...

Now. Oh *come on!* An army of kittens clawed the gullet at every fleeting thought of her absence, every unobserved effort ground away at the soul, no glory to be found, no fluidity of spirit, nothing. Head treacle oozed glacially, living each hour paralysed, looping in the emotional climax of a cheesy love song.

The situation proved too intense for my very little brain. Howling with loneliness in that cold, damp, putrified room, I cursed geography, the cost of phones, cost of travel, cost of platinum rings, pined for a close companion as a puppy might and, without really meaning to, began to mourn our relationship.

UNIVERSITY OF LOVE

5: Splurge

Determined to stop the rot, hardy bootstraps holding firm, plans went into overdrive to find an excess of pleasure that'd bring this unceasing barrage of gloomy gobbledygook to an end tolerably. Cider and cigarettes, the papers advertised credible things about liver and lung disease that I wanted to put to the test. I started saving the golden packets and stacked them up the wall with the intention of making a suit. The golden suit never happened, sad to say, I couldn't smoke enough, the stack of empty boxes stood only as a reminder of the money spent, how many metres of fivers burned away, however, I *did* make a golden top hat, with a plan of wearing it to house parties.

Parties, where real education happens, the best chance to shine, to display the true nature of the soul to pretty acquaintances, meet fellow students, prod and poke each other, debate the ins and outs of topics outside any comfortable frames of reference, and get so smashed that none could stand.

Armchair governors in waiting, waxy guests waned lyrical, playing the various vicarious victims to imagine what suffering might feel like, pompously advocating how life *should* be lived, how difficulties *should* be overcome, attempting to out-liberalise each other with ever-loftier opinions, pinning a close variance of a favourite parent's colours to some mast or other, questioning possible routes through very recently acquired knowledge.

In that harrying environment, loosened on economy alcohol, caught in a ceaseless torrent of righteous guff I cared not for, woeful tales of personal defilement would suddenly splurge forth in a morbid frenzy wholly unbecoming of a normal human being. Sadly, it appeared that my drunken self was intolerant of anyone who'd decided that they wanted to play the victim unnecessarily.

When intoxicated, the slightest thing could spark an episode as I'd filter everything through a victim's sieve in order to hammer any disagreeable lumps into a fine dust. Soberly accustomed to holding 'it' back, to keep 'it' hidden from view, I'd find myself waiting expectantly to use 'it' as a conversational weapon, a defensive trip-switch, a trump card of victimhood with which to beat away noisy people who pushed the buttons a bit too much. I became hardened to the sudden look of panic that would land as they'd scrabble for some soft platitude or other.

Usually, when it became known that I'd been dishonoured recently, in an unspeakable sense, most people would express pity, anger, and disbelief on my behalf. Though I didn't want pity and had plenty enough anger for us all. A big strapping lad like you? Yep, I was roofied. Oh? Yeah. Oh. Yeah. Oh! Yeah.

Parties, generally, aren't the best place for counselling, but people like to have a wild stab at it, to show caring. Bless 'em. Many males had stories to tell, but most didn't, lip-biting, fighting an inner-seal of confessional. Many females said that I was lucky not to have been impregnated, which remains a valid point, although, one could argue, not a very helpful point, at all, in fact, quite the opposite. When lump hammering, I could only hear of my 'good luck' from the mouth of an actual victim, not as petty point-scoring against *all* men, for *I'm* a man, and, yet, a victim. Empathy: Lesson five. Sympathy is not empathy. metoOmetoo.

After I'd been calmed and mollycoddled for a while, away from the group, it would often be difficult to return to the crowds, so, thanks, bye; quiet escape hiding the leaky eyes, pretending that another invite needed attending to, as the sea of eyebrows would rise in a tide to see the nutter safely out of the room.

Back to the shell. Back to the denial denying den. Back to the hell of myriad menial problems sobbing through the system, holding the head, moulding the bed, wishing for swift death, squeezing bodily liquids into thin loo-roll and pungent bedding.

As coping strategies went, while so determined to drink to demise, *attempting* to ignore 'it', but, in so doing, *failing* to ignore 'it', was no good for my health or for people nearby. My drunken self, a pitiable creature, could not be trusted to keep it shut. Bottling up thoughts through mindless distraction, and 'letting shit go', over time, had only served to fabricate a high-velocity cork of boozy botch and bungle. This wasn't peace. This wasn't harmony. This wasn't the joyful bettering of self that'd been promised by the carefree hippies I'd been trying to emulate.

A positive change of tact was needed to get 'it' out of the way, so that 'it' needn't come out later. I restrategised, telling people 'it' sober, out of context, at the first opportunity. Unsuspecting friends would introduce me to their friends, who would then either leave immediately with wrinkled temples, or would stand shaking their necks, tutting, which became extremely awkward for everyone, so that strategy bore no fruit either.

Disharmony seemed to be spreading all around me, from me, concentrically, and not *just* from experimental daily jazzing. Booze? Blame the booze. Silence swept through my heart again. Sobriety didn't cut it either, I really needed decent curative meds, a drug to help keep the wild creature inside hushed until death.

They call it dope for a reason. Grass, weed, bud, hash, whatever we could get, whatever was cheap, worked a treat. From a rich trombonist friend I borrowed: Vlad the Inhaler, a five-foot bong needing two people to work it, then set about keeping medicated away from the snooty gaze of party people. The beast restrained, the priest retrained, peace, love, laughter and patience returned. The daily grind had a smoother sanding-wheel installed, dreams became less stressful, acceptance of all things shitty became darkly humourous once more, people became less stressful too, distance passed under the feet quicker, life eased, all in all, I'd found my drug of choice. Thank you God for marijuana, please legalise it, and make it cheaper, Amen.

UNIVERSITY OF LOVE

6: Buddha and the Tortoise

Free living blew itself out almost immediately. The few quid available without effort had long ago been pissed up the wall or burned to ash, zero had become a long forgotten daydream; the bottommost reaches of sanctioned borrowing, a reinforced glass carpet, my form sprawled spread-eagle across it. All a loan did was pay off other debts, bought a lump, filled the fridge, and allowed for a few heroic nights of fiscally unfeasible wingmanship. Bills loomed ominously. Frugality reigned.

Big ideas of perishing bearably evaporated, sober penury coalesced. Dying young, in poverty, widely respected, that *was* still the only plan, but it wasn't as easy as it sounded, with cash so scarce, paid work so rare, and music *literally* time and effort. It'd have to be starvation or exhaustion, not drug-abuse, shame. Immortality on a compact disc would have to suffice for impact, all I now had to do was record the best jazz album ever, the more obscure the better, *then* die, *then* they'd be proud, or impressed, or sorry, or something. Admittedly, it wasn't a perfect theory.

Sculpting low frequency noise had the benefit of being a free pastime, moving about, however, became a problem, Yorkshire being only hillocks, hummocks and gradients. Shifting a double-bass and, often, large amplifier, around the city by foot was an exhausting, slow and smelly business. Buses were a luxury that 'wasn't beer', were generally insufficient for luggage needs, and full to the brim on rainy days. Taxis were right out.

In truth, the college *did* have some half-reasonable double-basses available, but college policy stated that a first year student wouldn't get a good one, and they didn't all have pick-ups, so *most* weren't band functional. Nor could a college-bass or amp be taken off of college-grounds. Bass-guitar? Um, no, thanks.

Inspired by skater housemates, when the last loan installment arrived, I invested in skateboard wheels, trucks, and bearings, attached them to the bottom of my combo amp with big screws, tied a headscarf around the handle and, with the bulky double-bass slung over the shoulder, wheeled it along like a play-buggy. It required torque to get moving, upward slopes troublesome, but with a bit of grit the city was mine to gig without the necessity of staggering back'n'forth carrying equipment being the only thing done all day. Sat atop the rolling amp, the double-bass held like a jousting lance, I'd ride any gentle slope. Gleeful. Genuine pleasure on tarmac. Paving and cobbles, much less so.

I'd found an identity: that bare-legged bloke with the double-bass, pit rings, and amp on wheels. Sure, I'd tried long trousers, but due to heat of effort burning muscles, legs would stream and steam on even the coldest, driest of days. Steaming legs cool more efficiently exposed. Plus, bare skin wipes clean after rain, whereas trousered skin remains soaked through. Shorts. Yeah.

Carrying burdens around everywhere took its toll. Hungry, tired, skew-whiff, smelly, shattered and semi-conscious all day, every day, after not very long at all the body started to break. If I'd known fatigue and blisters were prerequisites for a double-bass player I'd've learned the flute, but no one tells you that on the application forms. Sores, sciatic twinges, hobbling hips, weak knees, plantar fasciitis, verucas, styes, warts and gum-boils, the physique manifested the psyche, step by step by heavy step.

I'd disconnect from aches, float above the pain, enjoy the rain, ignore the physical strain, swing from a skyhook, imagining hosts of Holy angels raising me up. Detached from circumstance, from abrasions and bunions, from memories past, a new man reassembled every moment, I nodded and winked to anyone new, waved salutation to everyone I knew, mostly with a sweet smile and the lightest of dispositions, while trudging past sweaty, pained and gasping. Ahaha, yes, what a sight, I'm sure. Om.

One day, on my way through town with more equipment than a human should carry, I met a chap sat cross-legged on a traffic island crossing, he seemed nice, friendly, and so I plonked my stuff down next to him, above and around him. After ten long minutes of his sob story, I gave him a fiver, not much in the grand scheme of things, but several day's budget, and all I had.

I strode on, pretty chuffed with this new charity therapy, a wash of pure joy poured through me as I bounced down the hill. This feeling must be the Holy Spirit that I'd failed to find in church, I thought to myself, smugly. Letting go of the right things. Yay.

Next day, on the regular trudge into town with the double burden shouldered, I saw him exiting a large mansion house. He was wearing the grin of the sexually satisfied, had a four-pack of good beer tucked under each arm and was rolling a cigarette from a full ounce-pouch of tobacco. It seemed he'd had some luck. I hugged myself just a little bit, truly glad for him, pleased that happiness flourishes in the world if only one puts it out there, out there. Buddha would be happy, *pleased* even, Jesus too. Yay.

With a spring in my step, I waved, nodded and winked as we walked concurrently up to his gate. The very moment I opened my mouth to speak he asked if I had any cash, which I didn't, because I'd given it to him. He didn't recognise me. The double-bastard on my back didn't spark his memory. The hair, bleached and dyed funny colours by bored housemates, didn't trigger a single synaptic twitch. My telling him directly that we'd met yesterday brought only shakes of his head and a disdainful sneer.

As I shuffled off, he insulted selfish students discourteously and loudly at my back. I barely felt the leather strap biting into the flesh. Innate moralism pushed once more to its bitter edge, Buddha could fuck off; shells, staffs and soul-mates all.

I missed a valuable lesson that day. Playing the double-bastinado for a living is more strenuous and less profitable than begging.

UNIVERSITY OF LOVE

7: Help Desk

Each new morning, I would awaken anxious and miserable, evermore surprised by my continued pouting existence. If I had to consider myself one of the 'lucky few', as I'd been told I must, then the shit-bomb of corporeal reality for the 'unlucky many' *proved* the existence of a cruel and malicious deity.

One of the fortunates, here on a shared Earth, an equally vital fraction of humanity, or not, ready to make an equal share of impact upon this planet, or not, tick tock. Searching for calm ferociously, I had a really long hard look at myself, reaffirming physical persistence in the grotty bathroom mirror, a reflection of a shadow of a piquant man, under bad lighting, and yet, the occasional flash, a shiny twinkle of *something* behind the eyes. Hope? Wit? Cruelty? Malevolence? Stupidity?

Disquietening humours lay upon me, for the first time I *knew* that I knew nothing useful. Questioning all things only works if one asks the right questions. Finally, I admitted to needing help. In order to pass time constructively, I tracked down a student-run helpdesk for victims of rape, open for a few hours, once a week. I skipped a lesson and made the journey to see if they had anyone to talk to about quelling the appalling turmoil within, or, indeed, if I could help out at all making teas and coffees, and stuff. Having had some experience in these matters, I thought it would be nice to turn my hand to volunteering, to hang out, to join the crowd shouting about my own major topic of concern.

Upon arrival, the militant anti-man immediately suggested that I was there to 'turn myself in'. They were probably meaning to be funny. I didn't get it. In fact, I exploded in a violent rage, kicking up a rumpus like they'd never seen. I couldn't stop it. Hooooow? Fuuuuucking! Daaaaare! Yooooou?

The top blew off of my cranial thermometer. Irate, spitting with petulant incredulity through a watery blur, I demanded an apology, a written apology, not just from my accuser but from the head of the student body, the Dean, the Governors, the Chair of the university, the damned Secretary for Education. I wanted grovelling, I wanted it *here*, and I wanted it *now*, instantly.

At which, they stated quietly that they were sorry for the fact that I'd not had it explained to me how hard it was for women to have their safe spaces in the world, and, at length, that *that* office wasn't really the best environment for men, sorry, but you should leave, *now*, some of the ladies might feel uncomfortable.

My testosteronometer popped its gauge. Pupescent with rage, I stood quaking in my boots, grasping a pair of newly broken bootstraps, one in each tightly clenched fist. Daggers were glared and glared back, and glared again for far longer than intended, as a thousand nasty rasping thoughts failed to find purchase. Consciousness crumpled into a paper ball with all the precise words of rebuttal penned upon its hidden folds. Nnnnnnngh!

Calm. Calm! Public displays of angst and idiocy weren't in the master plan. Primary objective: to find a tolerable calm. Are you gonna leave, or shall I call security? Breathe. Breathe! Stammering something about 'it' happening to boys too, I stood clutching at my spiraling head, effing and blindly pushing out a tear or two, the sight of which brought a flicker of fretfulness, though far too late for me, flush with effrontery, I flounced off in a furious huff and a half, foaming with effervescent fury, following a famous formulaic format of shameful fuckwittery.

Hope remained that they *might* later feel guilty for misreading the situation so obviously and obliviously, and, therefore, *maybe*, might possibly treat the next male passerby with a little more respect, or less abuse, or not be so swift to judge, or something, but it seemed unlikely. *They* were why people *should* complain. If *they* represented *my* issues, then the system needed a reboot.

I hit a wall. There seemed little point going back or taking complaints further. They, for all their faults, were trying to help. Just because they couldn't help, and rubbed me up the wrong way, and then offended the very root of what I consider to be me, they hadn't intentionally meant any harm, they were just stupid, more stupid even than me, and yet, in charge of a help desk.

Maybe, just maybe, and no more, maybe I *couldn't* die just yet, *maybe* I'd like to leave the world marginally better than it was when I found it, *maybe* there could still be enough time to make a punctum on the infinite plane of existence.

Maybe, just maybe, if this unearthed charge of emotional static could be redirected to battle a deserved enemy, *then* life *might* be fruitful, even worthwhile, *maybe*.

Maybe taking up boxing would help alleviate some tension.

Maybe smashing fists against walls is a better, cheaper, more immediate alternative.

Maybe broken knuckles wouldn't help anything.

Maybe I should have thought about that earlier.

Maybe I did.

Maybe a major blood vessel will burst if ire fire flows unchecked for another single horrid minute, nnnnngh, maybe *this* minute, nnnnngh, maybe *this* one, nnnnngh.

Maybe by tomorrow it'll all be over and this will be the last thought I'll ever have, goodnight cruel world, oh, it's dawn.

A hapless mess of an exhausted man, I soon became my own super-anti-hero, with the classic useless alter-ego, triggered into action by raging injustice, the backstory wrote itself.

If you have a problem, if no one else can help, and if you can find him, maybe you can hire: Rapeboy, the victim's victim. Yay. Out for violent painful revenge should it ever happen to pass by. Give him a difficulty, and he'll stare out of the window, or at it, and pointedly try to think of something else, maybe compose a morbid poem, if he can hold the pencil in his mangled paw.

UNIVERSITY OF LOVE

8: Floristry

To repair my carbuncular soul, I required someone to hold, kiss, and share sunsets, now, tonight. Romance would save me. Reciprocated love. Sympathetic love. Passionate love. But, critically, most important of all, local love. If another perfect person came along to have luvvyduvvy conversations with, *then* there'd be a singular reason to blunder through each unrelenting, unremitting, remorseless, incessant bloody day.

Temptations of the flesh called loudly from women liberally distributed, and even though I kept my eyes to myself, or to other eyes, with hormones raging, synapses blazing, and sheer weight of numbers, I fell in lust hourly, finding no inner or outer peace because of it. Having told friends that I was taken, under assumption of harsh judgement, I started to regret that choice while lolloping about town with my tongue hanging out.

Thoughts of my officially unofficial girlfriend stayed my hand. I think, therefore: *blam!* Knots of self-loathing in the gut, clots of guilt in the mind. I didn't want to let 'us' down, yet I didn't want to die before popping that cherry. Dreams were as being stretched, squeezed and disemboweled by mad feral Banshees. Surely, a love shared is a love doubled, not a cold rejection of it, I'd try to convince myself, unsurely, but whether or not celibacy out-of-wedlock *would* or *wouldn't* guarantee entry into heaven, it is a matter of integrity. Virginity is a deeply scored barrier that one cannot cross twice, once across, there's no turning back, I wasn't truly convinced that I wanted to so casually toe that line.

Robbed of the mountings broody adolescence anticipated, occupied lamentably, lost amidst unceasing invasive onslaught. As at Dunkirk, ships had sailed, seamen backed up the lines, from Mardick, to Coxyde, rescue craft required directly.

UNIVERSITY OF LOVE

Amongst the general free-love meat market, which all of my housemates were enthusiastically making much loud energetic use of, I couldn't deny that I'd fallen for a fair few fair maidens, handpicked by eyeball for shared passions and likely reciprocal desires. Over time, improbably, several even warmed to me.

In university environs, with the music turned up fractionally too loud and everyone shouting at each other, hours wiled away intermingling with all, accepting of my purpose as wingman, distracting the insufferable, holding court to share a moan with the difficult. I was content, to a point; that adverse unhappiness that develops when drained of duty and obligation to platonic relationships with the spiritually misshapen. Enough is enough, ask anyone. Empathy: L6. Some people just won't fuck off. Omg.

Slyly, lying to myself, 'practicing', I'd wrangle my way next to favourite pretty people and, against God's will, boldly attempt to flirt, puritan style. Twitching neurons interacting with the most aesthetically pleasing in the room; fair forgivable flirtation, yeroner. I didn't know if they wanted me hounding them or not, I didn't much care, I was young, ebullient and maybe a bit tipsy, besides, I, myself, wished many people would stop bothering *me*. There's no variance of gender. No is no, thanks. Don't ask again. In a crowd of such lecherous activity, polite suggestion to meet up to get food together won over a few of the softer hearts.

Friendships would be built up slowly, then, at some point, loud tummy gurgles earned an invite to dinner, nudge nudge wink, bring pyjamas. The suggestions were apparently genuine. Vampires, thresholds, protocol. I made no similar offers. Mine? No. No way. No how. Not a chance. Not ever. Never. Nope.

I'd scrub myself salubrious, turn up with flowers and booze, eat, drink, stay up late nattering happily, playing games, I'd try my best to act distracting, charming, amusing, or whatever, until summoned to bed to 'sleep' for the night, as the boy chosen, from all other potential boys, to stay. Chip. Chip. Hooray.

Oh no. At the first offers I freaked out. Thanks for the food. Bye. Slam. Home, shell, bed. But, after one has kicked one's own butt in a lonely bed only a very few times, one learns courage. Learning how to say 'yes' began a new journey along a path of possibility, so bravely *would* stay over, but, typically, nary touch in anxious adjacency, as if an icy wind had chilled the soul.

After such nights, it seemed right to hug and nuzzle for a bit. We'd kiss softly, gently, shyly, slowly improving my technique, there'd always be a sexually quizzical moment of some sort to ruin. Then the moment would pass and we'd both know it. Okay, sleep well. Yeah, you too, *um*. What? Er, oh, nothing.

I'd made sure they were keen and single, made it painfully clear that I was keen and unburdened for what we had in mind, we'd put in all the hard work together, done the flirtation thing, played all the tricky games of modern humanity well enough to have found ourselves smiling across at each other in bed, yet, speaking for myself, I couldn't nudge any one of them 'over the line', nor, seemingly, would I be nudged, neither.

In such a world heaped with sexual expectations, and none, there can exist no precise way to evaluate what a woman expects from a man, or, more specifically, at that moment, from me. Probably nothing, as the feminists would quite rightly have it. No one wants the trouble of a pesky male bothering them when trying to sleep, I certainly didn't, and yet, as a pesky male, all that enwrapped every thought was how best to achieve orgasm.

A rutting man-boy in peak sexual prime, an alluring favoured physical form half-naked within arm's reach, filling the nostrils, there existed no other bio-chemical teenage focus. It felt to me, somewhere in the back and front of my mind, that our being there together had forced fate's hand, all I needed to do would be to let loose the beast and allow nature to speak its piece. But no. Courage lacking, I couldn't have been any more respectful if manifested as a potted funeral shrub in a smock.

Have they suddenly switched path? Have I? How do I find out? Is it because I've been acting weirdly? Am I acting weirdly? They *do* know I'm keen, right? Am I too keen? Have I let slip that I'm a victim? Did they find out from someone else? If so, who? Could they tell anyway? Is their acceptance of me based on sympathy? Empathy? Are they on a path to try to understand or repair me? What are they thinking? What are they thinking? What are they *thinking*? *Maybe* they're waiting for me to leave. Why can we not act upon something so likely to be beautiful? Could it be my ugly hands? Up close they were not a pretty sight.

My suppurated leprous hands weren't wandering anywhere. Unfortunately, pus-flushed flesh, blistered, popped and peeled fingertips were the bane of my love-life, or *a* bane. The double-bassist's curse. Unsmoothable skin edges would snag and catch sharply on nylon or polyester, or spandex, or silk, or satin, or lace, or anything that might ever be worn to please. Flesh on flesh fared no better, scritchscratching delicate areas as chemical stings of biological bustle burned the exposed hypodermis.

Not being a robot, and never wanting to turn away, I'd caress exposed flesh sensitively, with the back of a fist, in hope of recognition and reciprocation; it seemed rude not to after our fun-filled evenings. But. For how many seconds can one person touch another, without clear response, before 'affectionate' becomes 'creepy'? Not long in my mind. Maybe not at all.

Spooning became a cautiously chaste affair; under the false premise of thermo-cooling, I'd move my hips away from any close interaction to hide raging erections. Surely I'd get a slap and a lawsuit if I pushed contact in the middle of a cuddle without first getting married, or, at the very least, engaged.

Over and over, cursing shyness, querying every infinitesimal movement, spasms of intrusive thoughts were hidden by moving a pensive arm slowly, an inch at a time, to where it might rest, somewhere just beyond the bounds of open suggestiveness.

Muted alarm became sirens. Tender brain-cells flipped out. Empathy capacitors inverted. Bubbles of mind goo imploded. No precedent or justification could be found from first principles to action, for any action, whether that was as innocent as to cup a breast, or to merely suggest a late night activity to do together.

The main issue was that I didn't want to be seen to be manipulating the situation, yet obviously wanted to influence the outcome. I needed permission to act, but how to go about asking for it politely completely flummoxed me. I wasn't going to ask for anything directly with mouth words, in case an accusation of unseemly maneuvers could be leveled at me, for, to be seen to be wanting sex, by asking for it directly, would prove guilt of forethought, which was illegal for men, or heading that way, or something. Lacking for trust, the very idea of false accusations of unwanted manipulation filled the gills with terror. Thoughts of flirtations and intimacies misquoted as evidence of malintent by lawyers in a courtroom skewered icicles through the heart.

Yet here we were together in *their* bed. Could it be that it was *I*, *myself*, a dumb male, no less, being so wantonly manipulated? I'd heard that women could be clever like that, I was rather hoping, ears strained, tumid with anticipation. Maybe they'll offer themselves in a minute. Maybe I will. The mind whirred.

In those lonely moments spent together with familiar girls, I remember feeling envy for the club owner who'd had his fun, because at least he'd had the emotional wherewithal to act on his impulses. For good or ill, at least he'd actually done something in his sordid shitty life, I couldn't even frott properly with people who wanted me lying there next to them, who'd gone out of their way to make it happen. It seemed wrong that *he* should get to have the fun bit while catatonic nightmares of emotional castration filled *me* up. The animosity would build. Grr, I should never be thinking about him, the cunt, never, ever, never ever, never ever *ever*, *especially* not here in a girl's bed.

I'd lay there at a thousand miles an hour, like a head with the chicken cut off. Immobilised by philosophical plate spinning. Correct motivation to act 'properly' as a man in a feminised world, with dignity, integrity, respect, love, tenderness, and a healthy orgasm rate, still baffled and eluded me. Without diversion of some sort I'd only simmer, boil over, flinch and kick out, so, while distracting the brain from self-pity, I'd most often take this opportunity to dismantle the conception of whether 'inaction' could be a 'moral act' if initial intent had been to act immorally. Solace of some sort, I suspect. Judge, jury and executioner; self-convicted, heavily guarded, constrained, restrained and restricted by penal codes of cruel devising, loosely assembled from Biblical Scripture, the Laws of the Land, empirical data, Darwin, my mother, and a death wish; mashing them together confusedly, attempting the interminably toilsome task of unpicking a working ethics from the mindknot of a horny teenage brain in a single night, without reference books, while over-stimulated bodily, playing footsie, fighting back hormonal reality with the all too real threat of rape charges rarely out of the thoughts. This way and that. It probably wasn't the best time to start tackling such deep issues, but hey ho, gotta start somewhere.

The thought that my own invading manipulators would live forever in a similar jail of mind held some small comfort for me. I imagined maliciously that they'd wake up every single day crippled by the awareness that a well-placed phone call could wreck their names and lives in a finger-snap, that any day the full power of the judiciary could take away everything they love, dragged backwards through the courts for years. This horrid fear of sexual harassment charges hanging over them was their punishment from me. I reveled spitefully in how it felt so very *very* rotten. Good. And yet, self-punishment would only work if they held the same ethical views on what constituted acceptable behaviour as I did, which they most definitely did not. Bad.

With bottom lip quivering, I'd relive every second of my reaching manhood. All at once. Blam. And then again. I couldn't imagine a world where *all* men were required to be raped, to make them act flaccidly to women through a din of hateful memory and a hyper-empathic fear of future reprisal. It didn't seem a foolproof logic to be fed to schoolboys. It didn't seem like it could be rolled out nationally without somebody noticing and complaining. It still worked, sure, but entirely devoid of virtue.

The words didn't come, trailing logical threads were unclear, but somehow, deep down, I felt I'd justified it all by arriving back at the 'right' place anyway. Despite very best efforts, I'd reached puritanism via the back routes, emasculated by a brain full of contradictory rules and conflicted misunderstandings.

After much infernal debate, a draft conclusion found *all* glib sound-bitten advice to be insufficient to live by. Including that. Each individual word choice, stressful speculatively interpreted hyperbolic steps into a future memory-muddle of entanglement, parp, every original realisation accompanied by a discordant chorus of blaring tubas that'd wipe the mind clean of all mental constructs, to start building again from flashes, faces, phantasms, befuddled foresights, first and furthermost fundamental truths.

Truth? *Truth*? Bah. Mathematical certainty in set bounds, sure, absolutely, but a truth of words is almost entirely nonsense. Just because someone said something is so, doesn't make it true. Just because anyone says anything is so, doesn't make it true. Just because God wishes it, simply wasn't good enough reasoning any more, scripture didn't allow for the tweak of common sense. Just because the government, or a friendly hippy says so, wasn't entirely sound thinking either, on a whole variety of scale sets. Just because *I* say so, probably not. But why not? Reasons for laws held inside other heads were, what? Better than mine? Golden? Do as you'd be done by. Easy. I want sex, like every solitary ancestor ever did, even the particularly religious ones.

The minutes ticked by, unable to contextualise any of it. Hour. And a half. Two hours. And a half. Three. A dour huff would flare behind a clenched smile. Tensions would rise. Sleep? Not a chance. Where's my equilibrium? Where's my equiliberation? Calm. Cool. Cork. Quiet. Empathy. bOmb. Hmmmmm.

Turn away. Turn away. Okay, there we go, pressure off. Any moment now they'll spoon-cuddle *me*, any, moment, now. Now. Wow. A hand on the chest, briefly, pectoral muscles tensed hard. Hugging. Horizontal hugging. Why couldn't I yet instigate that easy thing? Why are tits so untouchable? Eh? Tit nipples. That's why. Tit nipples, bra-straps and fear. Fortissimo tubas to wipe thoughts away. First flash, face of effing arrrrrgh!

Impassive behaviour patterns, caused by bubbling internal conflict and over-thinking were a great contraceptive, probably for the best, criminal law blah blah blah, but, as a rutting male in the throws of heat, not really for the best at all. The end doesn't justify the means, when the means is tortuous turmoil, aching heart, insatiability, body and mind straining frustratedly at the failure to behave naturally, as a primate might.

While my housemates, and almost everyone else, were at it like lemurs; lawlessly, lechorously, lewdly, lengthily, loudly, limberly, luridly, lucidly, lovingly, luckily, liberally, liberatedly, and leaden-footedly, I required polite, slow, detailed explanation as to what I'd been doing wrong, some handy hints and tips to guide and instruct which idiosynchrasy to address in order to better my chances for next time. Yet, all pre-chewed sound-bites were insufficient, I'd progressed *that* far, seemingly backwards.

On the rare beautiful occasions my gnarly, rough, barnacled hand would be gripped and held warmly, delicate hearts would leap, at least a dozen of them in my chest alone, all clenched tensions would sag and slump immediately, allowing a relieved anxious little boy to drift off into the sweetest of dreams, connected in mind, soul, and spirit, a happy farty monkey.

The following day, the usual suggestion would be that I was gay, which stung a bit, but there you go. Too gay? Too feminine? Me? New ideas to absorb along with the deluge.

In the cold light of morning, it so transpired that half of them would've, if only I'd've asked, they told me so, in my guise as a probable gay, and I lost yet more sleep to kicking. In a race of one man, I'd managed to come in second, the only consolation found was in blaming *them* for *my* 'failures'; *they* didn't want *me*, *they* didn't push for it, *they* weren't in the mood, and *they* weren't responsive. Primary survival strategy as a rutting male: to remove self from failure. Likewise, half of them wouldn't've, which persists as a great reprieve all round, as far as keeping sex-offences off a criminal record for coin-flipping is concerned. Naturally, *I* didn't want *them*, *I* didn't push for it, *I* wasn't in the mood, and *I* wasn't responsive. Primary survival strategy.

I felt that I could've been trusted to leave these friends sexily unviolated without being trussed to solemn inertia by God, or His Laws, or any other imposed rules crowding in on personal and private interrelations, I'd've responded to 'no', the word is easy enough to understand, I'd become hyper-sensitive to it, but I hadn't thus far had a proper 'no' to respond to, I'd not yet created a situation where anyone had found the need to say it.

They probably weren't attracted to me at close-quarters, with smoky lager breath, wonky teeth, teenage skin, spots, shocking anti-humour, angsti-intellectualism, and natural odour exuding from the pores. That'll be it, *that's* much more likely, and fair enough, I couldn't possibly be *too* gay, could I? Not me, surely. Whatever, it needed correcting, so that I might lose my virginity before I died, by the end of the year, as promised.

Once or twice, invited back with expectation renewed, impetus regained, knowingly on a certain promise. Snap. Double the pressure, twice the failure. No breast cupped, no fanny felt, no erection pressed, nor sated. Not one 'no' needed. Not one.

UNIVERSITY OF LOVE

9: Defloristation

The final term arrived, still living in malodourous squalor, we had a party at our shitty house, which we'd prepared for by turning off the lights and turning up the music. I'm not much of a dancer, but was having a go, elbows jabbing this way and that, grooving to jazz funk fusion in my golden cigarette-packet hat.

Blotto, a girl grabbed my arm, dragged me to my rotting room and deflowered me. Scant memories include her fragrant hair in my face, the realisation that my only mix tape was extremely depressing, one long feeling of acute naked smelly shame, and a final vision of agonising pain, as of foxes shrieking in the yard.

A new dawn.

I awoke hungover, recoiling cerebrally in expectation of some divine vengeance, initially mortified for having directly violated God's will. I wondered in which way the world had now changed. Could people still see me? I hadn't yet any proof. In anticipation that I'd died, finally, I got out of bed just to make sure my body wasn't lying there motionless, remaining nervous that time itself had stood still, this room my personalised hell, I awaited angels to send me on a quest of retribution. She stirred, at least she's in this new world with me, maybe it's just us now. Sinners.

Door, hallway, all still there, nervous trip to the toilet, also still there, then back into bed to cogitate in fresh pants. As hours passed, nothing, or nothing else, other than a throbbing member, and a desperate replaying and patching together of fuzzy events.

People started banging about in the house. Reality continued. No thunderclap. No great fanfare. No displacement into a lonely universe. As I stared at the window, a flash of righteous fury overcame all else, stayed for a long while, and then subsided. Slowly, the heavy chains of ignominy fell from my shoulders.

By the time we got out of bed, childhood had become today's chip wrapper. Gravity had stopped working. She was smiling, laughing, and didn't hate me. Oh happy day. Rife was bliss.

I got overly keen and she snubbed me cold. For a few days my compunction sprung forth romantically under her window, until I saw a naked boy and ran away. Back in my shell was where I felt safest anyway. Dreams an odd lot, nightmares went crazy.

Life was bris. The fiery sensation below quickly developed into a volcano of intense pain, even in the loosest of cotton shorts. Elasticated underpants an absolute impossibility. It so materialized that *mutinium extremis* had been somewhat badly damaged in the scuffle. Maybe heavenly reckoning *was* due after all. Instant moral karma; nob-caned by a phallocentric divinity. I felt quite certain that God must be in the process of marking me impure with a deadly flesh-eating disease, one that would spread across the entire body intensely painful inch at a time, starting on the fore of phimotic foreskin, which burned to the tiniest touch, as dipped in chilli-oil, lavatory visits a most unpleasant surprise.

Time passed. Healing began, a mere flesh wound after all. Celestial meddling did not, in fact, manifest as a flesh-eating bug. Physically, I would repair, eventually, with balm, a great relief.

Internally, however, it was all kicking off. A life of fuming abstinence befouled of eternal perfection with my estranged gilt-edged girlfriend, for one short painful drunken experience and rejection, followed by a short painful penis, no erection. More distant from humanity than ever, this was not what I'd had in mind when I'd wished a 'sharing of love' into being; guilt, shame, physical pain, shimmering with fuck-it once again. In company; chipper, perky, *friendly* even, but, in the first instant alone, jittery, squawky and panic stricken. Everything out there, in its entirety, translated neurologically into how rotten *I* felt, *me*, a conduit for all the foolhardiness of the universe. Not one cell didn't loathe itself upon waking, surviving and passing out.

Unable to hide shame of dishonour, I started to inspect my ethics as one who'd lost his pure heart, as one whose destiny is certain. Hell it is. The futility of fated existence washed over me, as recognition of destiny does. Antagonised to death, and then some ill-described torturous hereafter, forever, until the rapture.

I'd begun to reimagine a one-size-fits-all pain-free afterlife, where ancestors await in full knowledge of shameful thoughts, the orgasm deal cut with God as a child, all of it. At death they'd wind back time and do a walk through, pausing and rewinding at all the bad choices to discuss what could've been done better, sitting through the tedious bits in real time, scrutinising masturbation techniques with a knowing eye, for aeons, and *then* reincarnation, or something. It didn't explain why the ancestors were there in the first place, but better than fire forever, *maybe*.

Divine violence's visceral vermiculation vaguely alleviated by vivisection of vain unheavenly values, how now, indeed, to make henceforward tolerable? If an afterlife reflected one's actions in this life, there'd be solace in integrity. In which case, for a happy ending, I'd have to own up, soon, before I died, it must be the next and last thing to do, a deathbed admission. Lying to myself and my parents, fine, but I couldn't keep lying to the girlfriend.

I called her halls every half-hour until she picked up, but then couldn't find the words. We agreed to meet up when we could.

At year's end, in July, the housemates headed homewards, as time was fit to do so. I stayed in that empty shitty house just as long as I could, hanging on to every blessed uninterrupted minute; sitting, thinking, contemplating, dawn to dusk, for the first time, not *having* to do anything or be anywhere for anyone.

A few good friends remained nearby; we cleared their freezers and watched crap telly in the peace of cynical laughter. The mind inflated like a weather balloon, to the size of a pea, as life's events flashed by for the last time. Contented, done, ready and waiting for death, any, moment, now. Now.   Now…

UNIVERSITY OF LOVE

Now nooooo oooooh ffuucckk.

UNIVERSITY OF LOVE

UNIVERSITY OF LOVE

pt.1a

Summary of Solipsism

UNIVERSITY OF LOVE

10: Gracelessland

Sussex called. Moving fun. Welcome home. Good to see the family. Shame to *still* be grounded. No cash, no access to cash. Get a job, here, phone, call the club. No, thanks. Why not, *lazy*? Um, er, om. Yellow pages, job agencies, the first A., interview booked, popped on down, promise of a job in a day or two.

Under that roof, I'd amends to make before family bonds could be sutured. I needed to serve my time, follow orders of progressive parental redemption, take their advice without lip, be useful, earn back respect previously lost being the family idiot, their strangely troubled youth needing to be tamed. Jump? Certainly, how high? No booze, no girls. Sure, oh, wait, what?

Home cooking choked in the throat, hard to swallow through a phantom desire for death by emaciation, which I'd hoped to overcome with access to food, but found I still had a real lack of hunger for. Let's say Grace. You know, I've suddenly lost all appetite to survive the day. Laughs couldn't be shared, tension vibrated along taut strings. Expectations of positivity were *so* manically high, as we tried to make the most of our short time together, that any speak of love had me running off for a cry and a rage, pushing blood to the head in silent screams for many many *many* minutes at a time. I guess I'd not really given up on the idea of a brain haemorrhage either. Come back to the table. Nnnnnngh, just a few more minutes, nnnnngh.

By personal choice, and yet, not by choice at all, lost, outcast and living in the wrong universe. I definitely didn't want to be such a little shit, so selfish as to reject lovingly prepared food and exultant talk of their loving God's love, but, while hiding the actual Devil inside, biting Him back, unavoidable reminders, such as prayer, set dying embers ablaze.

Oh, to feel that swim of family love, that spin of joy, when we'd stand together in church to sing lyrics praying for the rapture within 'our generation', and equally doomsaying stuff, happily, blissfully, ignorantly; before doubting a Protestant inheritance, before knowing what it meant to be labled w.a.s.p. as a bad thing by hippies, before querying scripture, which, even in private, still felt horrendous. With each new blasphemy came dizzying episodes, the emotional vertigo of sacrilegious detachment.

There were several lives required, a few just for me, a few for family, a split personality, if you will, as so many of us have, without the need to be diagnosed as having multiple personality disorder. More a multiple personality order, if anything.

A dull-eyed soft-spoken hipster, my main face, got on with day-to-day activities by autosuggestion and self-hypnosis. Duh.

A kind child would allow mention of Jesus' infinite love without smashing things, crushing down any disagreements into a singularity never to be dealt with in polite company. Om.

An old sceptic, taking notes; applying amateur scientific rigour to statements of scripture; storing questions to return to later when enjoying actual freedoms, away from religious absolutism pouring salt on all-purpose ethical cultivations; disdainfully taking scissors to the instruction manual of an amoral racist God one unnecessarily misleading statement at a time. Hmmmmm.

An erratic personality ranted, raved, ransacked rooms and struck rock hard walls in morbid self-awareness of stupidity, and in disbelief of such a widespread collective idiocy. Grrrrr.

Another squealy brain-squeezer would run away to cry. Wah.

Another would get any fatty food back up. Bleh.

Many more fragile states of mind delicately juggled, as is normal, all victims, all children, all grown-ups, all upset and anxious, all wishing for just enough faith to believe so as to be able to ignore restrictions in the physical world and revel in googoo-gaagaa blup blup bang shooey as the truly religious do.

Unhappily, no faith could be found, I wasn't in the business of giving up my new set of partial-liberal-worldly-truths only to faithfully return to the more familiar sets of known lies, for there were one or two difficult 'facts' that superseded all pertinent religious exceptionism. Upon this topic, my minds were as one, one big mess, a contrarian teenager, splintered into fragments, living a shocker, needful of love, knowledge, a sulk, and therapy.

The ban on criticising religions and the religious stood as law, *especially* in that house, but widely too. I couldn't help but think that religious recrimination and a few home truths would be just what billions of sensitive idiots, such as myself, required.

Surely, any good Protestant should protest? Yes? Yes. But, no. Not me. Not to the parents. I yearned to tell them that their God's blessings weren't all they'd claimed them to be, yet, mind-knotted, kept most of the biggest questions to myself.

So, if 'our' 'Lord' is so loving, and we're going to talk of 'Him' as the Holy Trinity, 'Them' no less; where were 'They' when I had a dick up my arse? Was I touched by the hand of the Lord Himself? Was it a transubstantiation of Holy Spirit that I wiped off my leg? What *purpose* has a Being, who receives thanks for intervening, but never intervenes? Superior moral guidance? Since when? Gay rights? Ah, Jesus Christ Emmanuel. Child abuse? Ah, Lordy. Why am *I*, of all people, more accepting of homosexuals than the scriptures? Fundamentally, all religions start with scripture, scripture is homophobic, factually, so, in a world of equitable equality, aren't Liberal Christians a paradox by very definition? Isn't 'personalised-religion' a failure to observe 'Holy-decree'? Feminism: or, an unknowable, ineffably homophobic God? Either: one, or the other, is that really a life choice? Seriously? How to reveal the mind of such a God? Exorcism? Would one need to be a vicar? An atheist? Both? Is it legal to renounce a family Church publicly? Refute a God-given heritage? Is it *illegal?*

Moot muted contentions.

Asking for a friend, I set up some moral mysteries for the parents to tackle, much in the manner of the vicarious victims I so reviled, to allow opportunity for the best of their thoughts to be given a fair airing, that I may glean the right kind of advice. We discussed the carefully chosen subjects cagily, until clichéd logic bubbles popped out. I remember most: forgive and forget.

Forgive and *forget*. I shall *never* forget that, *unforgivable*.

Forget? Fuck off. Things need remembering, not forgetting. It's entirely backward and inverted. Shall we forget our lessons? Our growth? Our scars? What'd be the point of learning *then?* What would be the point of anything if, as soon as it happened, we went out of our way to wipe it completely from our minds? Lest we forget, wars, what are they good for? Remembering. Not to glorify, but as a reminder that we shouldn't go down that terrible path again. Active forgetting? Not the greatest advice. But where *is* the good advice? Which sacred words hold 'truth'? In a sprouting intellect it isn't feasible that one *could* know what to forget when so much is learnt from studying peripheral facts, then altering, adapting and supplanting the slew of new pieces onto muddled or empty mind-maps. Here be dragons. Forget all, but for that which we instruct you; don't just hide your light under a bushel, put *your* light out, take *our* light, spread *our* light. Here be goldfish happinesses and ingrained parrot effluent. Without a reliable cross-cultural guidebook, interpreting the conflicting truth claims is an impossibility, as is the case with; science and religion, secularism and religion, law and religion, capitalism and religion, communism and religion, literature and religion, every 'true' religion and any single 'true' religion. *Forgetting* rival truth claims reinforces mythical beliefs: mythiefs, if you will. I wasn't gonna have my experience stolen from me. Besides, to preserve my own various sets of lies, I needed to remember everything, *every* little thing, every single tiny little bloody thing, sharply, acutely, microscopically, by necessity.

Forgive? Koff. Oh to be of such a skywards state of mind, so elevated, so freely able to take laws unto oneself to pronounce judgement upon another's behaviour, or one's own behaviour. Oho, here we go, I'm forgiven am I? *Yes, you're forgiven.* Nice, thanks, so, *muggins*, the action that offended enough to merit forgiveness didn't injure sufficiently to form a lasting grudge, great, well, expect those behaviours again, and worse, and soon, as the kind of person who obviously tries to forget things too, you daft *mug*. Forgiveness *too easily given* is a let off. It's not your fault, you're freed from the consequences of your actions, you weren't to blame. That's how all-too-easy forgiveness goes. To *qualify* for *real* forgiveness, from within or without, desire to behave 'better' *than a previous incident* must be shown to be processed, acted upon, and proven over time, and yet, *and yet*, 'f.&f.', frequentative fungible flub, 'f.&*fucking*f.', for forlorn fools to fuddle and fudge, as fits the foot. Once sound-bitten, twice shy, thrice shite, try *that* for size. Turn the other cheek? Are you mad? Terrible advice. Sadist advice. A tooth for a tooth, is a valid truth too, let's have a piece of *that* action, I'll bring the broom handle. Is forgiveness to be forced upon me and mine, due to family claims that the justice of the NT supersedes the justice of the OT? Am *I* a mug? Are my *family* mugs? Are *all* good Christians mugs? How does one find out? Who speaks for Christians? *God*? Yes? Through scripture, directly? No? Through just the one church? No? Only prayer, directly? Oh. Then, are *you* a channel to God? Are *we*? Are *they?* Are *your enemies*? Do *we all* speak for God? Just those representatives that *you* agree with *currently*? Really? Reheheheally?

Well, fine, if forgiveness is more important to our society than retaliation, that we may continue forgetting those in our midst who quite literally need to be educated in right and wrong, fated as creed instructs, here's my cheek, jutting, proudly defiant, sucked up and stuck out, ready for someone to knock out a truth.

Whatever it is that troubles you, Jesus washes away your sins, but wherever He'd washed mine, I wanted them back. I needed to suffer, wallow, sift through my 'sins', to separate right from wrong, compare and contrast, dissect, scrutinize, understand mistakes with no excuses, no demons to take the fall, no unseen forgiveness thrust upon anyone, for *any* reason, ideally. When the claim to moral authority is exigent upon an unprovable mind in Man's invisible image, such an act of hubris, as to forgive on God's behalf, is no more than an empty decree, public shaming delivered by an arbitrary community of localised curtain twitchers.

Awhirled of indifference, with the yes yes mentality of regret, as from one who owed, and will forever owe, a debt of life itself to the parents, I found myself sat on their floral-patterned couch, saddened, confused, envious of their easy love, mulling the tree of knowledge of good and evil, godly lies and serpentine truths, slow-stirring over-emotionalism to calm, thick, brain-custard, unable to remove the frown from my fretful face for family photos as famous effing phrases fermented and fomented fruitlessly, fundamentally unenlightened in a world of difference.

Obliged of love, food, roof, bed, I still didn't want anyone's haughty damn forgiveness, and yet, and yet, they *were* correct, f.&f. happens naturally in a tired brain. One simply cannot maintain a pure concentration of hatred at all times of the day and night, if, say, blood sugar is low, or if, half of the time, problems remain unspoken behind other daily issues.

There were only a few people who I felt truly superior to. Fuckers. Ironically, they were the only people in the universe capable of having my forgiveness thrust upon them, and so they got it, they actually got it, or something that felt very much like it, as a part of humanity, part of a hierarchy of decency, an end link added to the chain of common courtesy. *You're* better than *me*; more knowledgable, wiser, but *I'm* better than *them*, *they're* scum, and they'll have to live with that forever and ever. Amen.

A handful of moral high ground still existed below, if I hauled up my mass and squeezed their vile spirits into the infinitely thin crush above rock bottom. In dreamscape's rush, they fell at terminal velocity within my inertial reference frame, close enough to swim over and reach out to slap and punch their hideous daemonic faces in frenzied ferocity, to kick their killed corpses into the horizon of a super-massive black hole.

Wrestling blankets, I'd awake exhausted, allow fury to flourish physically on the alarm clock, take a brief moment for a few deep lungsful of reality, take stock of who I'd be lying to today, then, newly reminded of which threads of sanity to cling to, cool, slowly, to keep the silent peace, such as it was.

Deceptions *had* to endure to avoid upheaval, but those days did not pass quickly, acting the act of false penitence: fenitence, if you will; eagerly enduring the disciplines of the wrong behavioural issues' needless correction, in the wrong person.

Vengeful hush was a bullet in the foot, for having 'forgiven' my trespassers, taking the law into my own hands, judgement away from family, friends, police, and courts of justice, I'd given up on all protections the country could provide, and yet could never provide if I wouldn't testify. And I wouldn't, as Jesus wouldn't. Whilst *not* being crucified to painful death for the sins of strangers, at least, I'd still accepted the sovereignty of *all* sinners, as Jesus had taught, as couldn't be unthought. *My* secret, *my* path to piety, *my* hidden power, *my* victimhood, *my* solipsism, *my* myopia, *my* blindness to public responsibility. Mine. All mine.

Fearful that a fierce fenitent duty too far might finally force fate's hand to defy insufferable fortune and finger the fuckers; willfully finish foe's futures; it crossed my mind, maliciously, that the act of 'retrieving the soap' mightn't be so much a horrifying ordeal, as a busman's holiday. Contemptible, hateful, but solace, of a sort, backing my inaction with rationale found slithering cowardly 'neath obelisks of forced forgiveness.

And so, sordid lies continued, and continued, and continued, and continued, and carried on, and on; the guilt, false guilt: fuilt, if you will, the fenitence and follity also. Having it both ways, all ways, every way. Controlled chaos, but without control.

The mind needed to be trained away from holes of thought, but reminders attacked from everywhere. Adverts, for example, in liberal England, don't have women's nipples in them, yet plenty of topless men. It is only a short paranoid hop to thinking the world is set up purely for the satisfaction and sexual gratification of straight women and gay men, and another short hop to feel resentful about it. Oh, the irony. Naked men, persistent as a traumatic image on the retinas, a subjective set of abhorrent images to trigger morose antagonism: mantagonism, if you will. I didn't want to see topless men's nipples on adverts, or album covers, or packaging, or men, or me, or anywhere at all, public places generally, the very sight taking resentful thoughts down the slippery slides to recall and rumination of dark matters, staring at eternity through any cosmos getting in the way. Immediate, intense flashbacks of flesh violation, sympathetic pains not uncommon, in some circumstances there is no choice but to curse and shake helpless fists at the sky. Constipation, for instance, torment. A life sentence, unable to clench buttocks around a hard stool without shadows darkening an already strained mood.

Drawing up blueprints for magnificent escape, it had crossed my half empty glass darkly that I might want to take someone down with me when I go. Yikes. That's not a path to inner peace. *That's* downright evil. The repaired bootstraps that I'd been tugging so hard at had begun to give out weakly at the eyelets. Poor little old me. Woeful, beyond description or prescription. Drowned in tearful pity puddles, despair smothered every spare unmedicated juddering shuddering second. Better bootstraps required, but, *still*, good to be home.

11: Heartbreak Hole

So where *was* my girlfriend? Next time we were to speak face-to-face, in *any* circumstance, I'd tell her the explicit truth about stuff, *all* of it, the complete package, as practiced on so many pained nights. Apparently, I needed her to forgive *me* my trespass of adultery against *her*, if we could only talk it out.

Well, once I'd promised my parents that I wasn't going to meet up with her, I got approval to use the landline to phone her. I managed to ascertain that she'd moved out of her halls, so stopped calling there. I phoned her parents house, hoping that's where she'd be, only to find out that she'd decided to stay in Scotland for the summer, working through, independent, far far *far* away. This devastating news, funnily enough, combined with house rules, trickled like water off of a duck's back, into a gaping hole. Her parents said that they didn't know her new number, which I didn't believe. By the third or fourth time pushing for it they stopped answering calls, instinctively protecting their little girl from the madness of a legally proven idiot. I only want to split up, you'd never have to see me again, don't you *get* it!? No, they didn't *get* 'it', but, ready to pop, I wasn't going to be splurging my troubles to her parents *first*, not for access to a useless phone number; not after so long waiting to have that heart-to-heart with my loved love, just to waste it on *them*. No.

The option to speak face-to-face had been taken away, so, one might think that *that* solves *that*, yes? Yes. But, no no no no fucking no, it seemed we were destined to be together forever, only, distant, and entirely uncontactable. I couldn't take any more shite, I was full. Decided, once again, but with zero doubts, though I couldn't tell her, or even leave a message, it was over. It was all over. Done. Dusted. God would have to bloody tell her.

UNIVERSITY OF LOVE

12: Working it out

I don't have a problem, I don't have a problem, *really* I don't. Caught in loops of dumb thought-bottling and panicky defeatism I'd settled back into drinking any booze I could lay my hands on, against the rules. There was never quite enough in the room to satisfy the desire to be slightly drunker than this. Sadly, alcoholism comes at a price: the very real cost of money.

The rules stipulated that to leave the house alone, there must be work booked to go to. So, I worked and worked, and always insisted on walking myself home. Slip slip away. Sip sip hooray. And rum for luck. Pip pip can't stay.

For cash, evenings passed in theatre pits playing the double-bass for amateur-dramatic shows that previous connections had got me in on. These shows weren't good earners, running for a week or two, paying roughly for themselves in terms of nightly interval drinks and after-show drinks, and pre-show drinks.

Daytimes were spent at the whim of the alphabetically blessed job-agency, with the tanned beauty behind the desk whose heady perfume melted any full-blooded male into their chair. If there *were* any work, they'd call early on the landline, the other end of the house. Keen to get out, I'd sleep on the stairs near the telephone in hope of leaving the close confines of the big airy house in hope of booze. Financially, they promised more than a pint an hour; I kept an eye on the clock, counting the minutes, licking salty lips, mentally measuring volumes.

They found work sweeping the town rubbish-tip, which I loved, pushing the broom up and down, getting the place clean, poking around in the mucky brass for little gems and keepsakes. I found a working cornet and a snare drum that needed new lugs, but, bottom of the pecking order, the foreman took them home.

They found work in a laundry, folding wet sheets on the sheet-drying-and-folding-machine, with a clicker to count how many sheets had been folded, easy. It wasn't hard to beat the numbers daily, causing irritation and resentment in the lazy mentally deficient foremen. A tiny cold-war was fought. Bye.

They found work adding cod-fat to pork shoulders for Christmas hams, which was fine, as one of few English speakers relaying the foreman's requests by first action, proudly was I given charge of the electric pallet mover, which I managed to reverse into myself, crushing my knee. I never told anyone, but confirmed myself to be a pillock. A lop-sided limping pillock.

They found work kitchen-portering in a chain-store café, which was brilliant, alone with thoughts needing to be thought, ensuring every single little thing in the entire place had been steam-washed, which is great for metal teapots and ceramics, but awful for raw fingertips weeping into communal marigolds.

They found work on the bin lorries, which is hard work, very *very* hard work, punctuated with two hours doing nothing travelling to and from the landfill, drinking booze and swearing.

Day one, sent home to get better footwear. Footwear bought.

Day two, survived, hard graft achieved with positive attitude.

Day three, weak chest had frozen solid, back too, I couldn't roll over, cramps in every appendage, bed agony the only option.

Day four, the pain changed, worsened, bed rest continued.

Day five, protesting physical work at the agency office, the chair-melter wouldn't offer anything else if I wouldn't complete their contracts seriously, so, I did a few push-ups and went back to the bins on a fitness tip, but lasted only a few days. Powdered rubber gloves reacted with open blisters, pulled muscles from palms to chin to ankles sending shockwaves up nerves on touch, broken glass scratching gouges through trousers, spray in mouth, feverish infection, ache without respite was too much, I broke.

Right. Okay. Decision time. Death, or better life? Which is it?

After all things, tax-payers were funding my training as a double-bass player, it would be no more than a direct insult to every hard-working person in the country if I continued purposefully damaging hands and body for a few measly quid, having been given such a glorious opportunity to raise expectations through a good education, or near enough, on paper, at least.

Following the principle that if you *demand* better for yourself, you'll get better, I *insisted* on some less-physical work from the agency, overcoming her exotic love-potion with teenage gusto, at which, they immediately didn't find any work for a dry week.

Eventually, they found work as a barman in a *fairly* swanky hotel, when, after a few hours of happy polishing on best behaviour in a black bowtie, a large bearded bully sacked me for wearing a 'scruffy' cotton shirt. He let slip how much the hotel paid the agency for staff at the top of his booming voice, I let slip my hourly rate in reedy self-pitying tones; his thundercloud stopped flashing, slowed its broiling, then dissipated, slightly.

The agency was taking eighty percent. Eighty. *Eighty* percent. Let me repeat that: eighty. The agency were *knowingly* taking eighty percent. *Before* tax. A major shock to us both. We stood blinking for one and two and three and four and five and six and seven and eight and nine and ten and eleven and twelve and thirteen and fourteen and fifteen and sixteen and seventeen and eighteen and nineteen and twenty, about twenty one seconds, speaking volumes with eyebrows and the occasional glottal stop, then stormed off furiously in opposite directions, I, as was my wont, stopping sneakily somewhere secret on the path home for a swift soothing snifter.

I stopped working for the agency, bunch of crooks, instead, continued playing bass at the theatres and, in the last weeks of the holiday, painted the car port, for my father, for hard cash; the paint brush like sharp lava in the paw. The short sober walk to the bedroom allowing for zero sneaky alcohol whatsoever.

UNIVERSITY OF LOVE

13: Brewer's Droop

At the very end of the holiday there was a get together for old tertiary college friends, a birthday or something. I worked hard for permission, then took the train, early, cost be damned.

A crowd appeared. We drank and drank, and we didn't care. Old friends sat around chewing the fat, pondering those who couldn't make it, loved ones lost, like attending a funeral wake, but with the debatable reprieve of not being a corpse.

People dribbled home slowly as last trains came and went. Personally, I was so contentedly out of it, so glad to spend a night away from sobering restrictions that I'd made quiet plans to out-party everyone, be the very last one sat on the bench outside the kebab shop, and then go from there. Or stay there.

At the very end of the night, one other, a girl, had also outlasted everyone and there we were, sat on the bench in a happy silence staring at the greasy people. She: a playmate in orchestras, a stunner, flowers in the hair, surfer chick cool. We'd flirted before, doing bad capoeira in sunny fields. She held my arm warmly; I started crying uncontrollably, a passionately sad drunk.

Against my better judgement, I stood up, ranting and raving about the stresses of life, the constraints imposed upon us all, how simple it would be if we all gave up vain hopes of ambition and lowered our expectations to the point that the inefficiencies of a musician would become valued more highly, and similar. Animated, gesticulating wildly, tears rolling chinwards, arms swinging madly, proposing that I'd give it all up tomorrow if it meant a guaranteed future with happiness at the end of it, oh, that it were ever so simply done! When, suddenly, she jumped up, grabbed me, kissed me, and said, breathlessly, that I would be sleeping with her that night. Er, okey-doke.

We walked off with some difficulty, staggering down the hill hugging, kissing, and really getting into it. She grabbed my arse, I grabbed hers and recoiled, she laughed and pushed back roughly; bracing me against walls, lifting a leg between mine with an anatomist's knowledge and succubus' intent. Marvelous.

A fitness fanatic, her body hardened by energetic activity, keen on bear hugs, she squeezed out more chemical electricity in those blessed minutes than in a frustrated lifetime before.

God owed me this. All I'd ever desired was this unbridled permission to hold and connect, it could all be so very simple. Life seemed so abundantly vibrant, my path had become so perfectly well defined. I needed this woman in my life.

Unyielding from the moment we'd first kissed, I stood at full salute as we stumbled into her place. We had to be quiet. Really quiet. Accidentally bumping into walls and knocking over vases, catching on the steep stairs, we made it to her loft after much stifled laughter and frolics, then spent a few minutes on top of each other, rubbing, squirming and intertwining, quivering with sexual expectation. We started undressing each other, desperate to be naked, pulling at difficult buttons, straps, toggles, clips and mechanisms. The shorts were off in a second. Shorts. Yeah.

She went to do something important briefly then returned to jump my bones but, in those few short minutes, the beer had come back to bite me, and her. She fell on the floor in a crumpled heap more than once, simply from perching without a sturdy pole to stabilise herself. We laughed and shushed and laughed some more, but my little man had given up and there was no reviving him. *She* persevered, which filled me with impotent glee and haunting visions of perfect failure forever, but when I suggested that, for the sake of further embarrassment, we have another go in the morning, she kindly agreed. Lying side by side, we drifted off into smiley sleeps the both of us, spooning tightly, I, defiantly cupping an athletic breast and most exquisite nipple.

In the morning, a single crusted eye peeled open to take stock of the day. She: as naked as a flame. Gorgeous. Stunning. Superb. I'd never seen such athletic perfection in my brief, closeted life; I smiled and stirred under the bed-sheet with pure chemical readiness within, blood-flow surging through youthful loins.

In the soft gooey viscosity of morning syrup, fortified by togetherness, where doubt and worries had been, strength itself stood glowing. King and Queen of all we surveyed, lustrous imaginings lifted our spirits up into the sky; floating, up up up, led by wanton desire, enwrapped in warm cotton-wool clouds we drifted across the fluffy dreamy effulgence of a viridescent mountain kingdom to the open balcony of a tall fairytale tower, light stone walls, amber lit in burnished pastel hues of dawn, ringed by suits of ancient armour that crumbled at a glance; an imposing four-poster bed, slung satin, crisp linen, rose petals, touching each other in roiling perfection of romantic unity, combined adoration, heart's intent pushed into every capillary, orgasmic to the touch, squidgy tentacle tessellations thrubbed pulses of interdimensionality from jelly neck to diamond-tipped phallus, to belly, to brain, to balls, skin prickling with delight, every smile a great wash of joy, turned inside out and tickled with feathers by a teddy in a dress, alone together, soaring high over twinkling landscapes, up up up, accelerating, up up up, into cold thin air, up up up, silk sheets buffeting in our wake.

Up up up, I gotta go. *Uh?* Wake up sleepyhead, I let you sleep, but now I gotta go. *Wha'?* I gotta go, you gotta go, we gotta go. *Oh*, googoo, c'mere f'ra shnurgleurglemmhmmm. No, now.

A repeeled eye took in her clothed form, dressed to the nines. Glorious. But what was that you were saying? *Whatever* it was, she needed to leave, with barely enough time to grab the shorts from the floor and take a push in the back out of the front door.

We were walking in different directions; I went and got a train. On the train, I realised that I didn't have her phone number.

www.ingramcontent.com/pod-product-compliance
Lightning Source LLC
Chambersburg PA
CBHW061340040426
42444CB00011B/3016